Edward Sandford Martin

A Little Brother of the Rich

And Other Poems

Edward Sandford Martin

A Little Brother of the Rich
And Other Poems

ISBN/EAN: 9783744705240

Printed in Europe, USA, Canada, Australia, Japan

Cover: Foto ©Thomas Meinert / pixelio.de

More available books at **www.hansebooks.com**

A LITTLE

BROTHER OF THE RICH

AND OTHER POEMS

BY E. S. MARTIN

NEW YORK
MITCHELL & MILLER
28 WEST 23D STREET
1888

CONTENTS

CONTENTS

A LITTLE BROTHER OF THE RICH.

TO put new shingles on old roofs;
    To give old women wadded skirts;
To treat premonitory coughs
    With seasonable flannel shirts;
To soothe the stings of poverty
    And keep the jackal from the door—
These are the works that occupy
    The Little Sister of the Poor.

She carries, everywhere she goes,
    Kind words and chickens, jams and coals;
Poultices for corporeal woes,
    And sympathy for downcast souls;
Her current jelly—her quinine,
    The lips of fever move to bless.
She makes the humble sick-room shine
    With unaccustomed tidiness.

A heart of hers the instant twin
    And vivid counterpart is mine;
I also serve my fellow-men,
    Though in a somewhat different line.
The Poor, and their concerns, she has
    Monopolized, because of which
It falls to me to labor as
    A Little Brother of the Rich.

11

For their sake at no sacrifice
   Does my devoted spirit quail ;
I give their horses exercise ;
   As ballast on their yachts I sail.
Upon their Tally Ho's I ride
   And brave the chances of a storm ;
I even use my own inside
   To keep their wines and victuals warm.

Those whom we strive to benefit
   Dear to our hearts soon grow to be ;
I love my Rich, and I admit
   That they are very good to me.
Succor the Poor, my sisters, I,
   While heaven shall still vouchsafe me health,
Will strive to share and mollify
   The trials of abounding wealth.

BALLADE OF THE GENERAL TERM.

E ACH in his high official chair ;
    One who presides ; two plain J. J.
Decent of mien and white of hair
They sit there judging all the day.
The gravity of what they say
Bent brows and sober tones confirm ;
Brown, Jones and Robinson are they,
Justices of the General Term.

I see the learned counsel there
Rise up and argue, move and pray ;
Attorneys with respectful air
Their legal acumen display.
Serenely joyous if they may
Of justice keep alive the germ ;
Motion and argument they weigh
Those justices of General Term.

That court I haunt, not that I care
For Justice in a general way;
Nor yet because I hope to share
With anyone a client's pay.
The reason why I there delay
And on the court's hard benches squirm
Is that of Love I am the prey—
Her father is the General Term.

I look at him with dire dismay—
Scorched by his eye I seem a worm.
"Dismissed with costs," is what he'll say—
That Justice of the General Term.

INSOMNIA.

COME, vagrant sleep, and close the lid
    Upon the casket of my thought:
Come, truant, come when thou art bid,
    And let thyself be caught.

For lonely is the night, and still;
    And save my own no breath I hear,
No other mind, no other will,
    Nor heart nor hand is near.

Thy waywardness what prayer can move!
    Canst thou by any lure be brought?
Or art thou then like woman's love
    That only comes unsought?

INFIRM.

"I WILL not go," he said, "for well
    I know her eyes' insidious spell,
And how unspeakably he feels
Who takes no pleasure in his meals.
I know a one-idead man
Should undergo the social ban,
And if she once my purpose melts
I know I'll think of nothing else.

I care not though her teeth are pearls—
The town is full of nicer girls !
I care not though her lips are red—
It does not do to lose one's head !
I'll give her leisure to discover,
For once, how little I think of her ;
And then, how will she feel ? " cried he—
And took his hat and went to see.

A PRACTICAL QUESTION.

DARKLY the humorist
    Muses on fate ;
Ghastly experiment
    Life seems to him,
Subject for merriment
    Sombre and grim ;
Is it his doom or is't
    Something he ate ?

15

CRUMBS AND COMFORT.

L ET no man, irked by tedious fate,
   The worth of victuals underrate;
But thankful be if so he may
Environ three square meals a day;
     For, barring drink, there's naught so good,
     Up to its limit's edge, as food.

Up to its limit? Yes, but will
Food satisfy as well as fill?
Hear humankind responsive groan—
" Man cannot live by bread alone!"
     Oh, tell me, Sibyl, tell me whether
     A man might live on bread—together!

ASHORE.

Man's happiness depends upon the views
He takes of circumstances that he's in.
To some it is a greater joy to lose
Than it, to others, ever is to win.

SINCE our poor hopes, like vessels tempest tossed,
Are duly wrecked, and all illusion ceases;
Now that the game is up, let's count the cost,
And estimate the value of the pieces.

And first, our heart : It was a flimsy thing
Already when we dared this last adventure :
And if it's flimsy still—Why, that should bring
No added liability to censure.

A serviceable organ is it still,
That does our turn in absence of a better;
And very shortly, we believe, it will
As calmly thump as though we'd never met her.

If tissues are so delicately spun
As not to stand a reasonable racket,
Their anxious owner has as little fun
As Master Thomas in his Sunday jacket.

Give tender hearts to those who like that kind,
And gain in strength with every pang they suffer ;
We praise that sort, but with relief we find
That ours is tough and yearly growing tougher.

17

Our head remains the same indifferent pate,
  Guiltless alike of learning and of laurels.
We notice, though, with thankfulness, of late
  A measure of improvement in our morals.

Our purse was always lean, so it amounts
  To little that it yet remains depleted ;
Though florists' and confectioners' accounts
  Are in, and payment of the same entreated.

We've lost a heap of time, but being rid
  Of time, one always gets along without it.
Could we have spent it better than we did ?
  Another might ; but, for ourself, we doubt it.

And we have learned—nothing. We knew before
  The folly and the vanity of wooing ;
And if we chose to try it still once more,
  'Twas not to win, but simply to be doing.

It was not that we hoped to gain a heart ;
  That that were vain required no further proving.
It only meant that souls that live apart
  Yield sometimes to the human need of loving.

Is this the last ? While yet his garments drip
  The stranded mariner forgets his pain,
And rescuing the remnants of his ship,
  Already plans to make them float again.

BARTER.

YES, there's a hole; you needn't be
    At pains to point it out to me:
        I know it.
I do not claim the piece is whole,
Or that its yard of width is full:
        I merely show it.

Fast color? Do I really think
That being soaked it will not shrink
        When dried?
Now that I've got it off the shelf,
You'd better test the dyes yourself,
        And so decide.

Cotton? I dare surmise it's full
Of threads that one might wish were wool,
        If wishing did it.
Look sharp; but if through being blind
Some flaw or fault you fail to find,
        Don't say I hid it.

The price is high. You think it so?
Well, this is not, I'd have you know,
        A bankrupt sale.
These wares of mine if you despise,
Some other dealer's merchandise
May find more favor in your eyes;
To hold mine over for a rise
        I shall not fail.

BEGGARS' HORSES.

I WISH that altitude of tone,
   The waistband's due expansion,
The faculty to hold one's own
   In this and t'other mansion;
And shirts and shoes and moral force,
   Topcoats and overgaiters,
Were things that always came of course
   To philosophic waiters.

I wish that not by twos and threes,
   In squads and plural numbers,
Young women would destroy one's ease
   Of mind and rout one's slumbers;
But that if by a poor heart's squirms
   Their pleasures know accession,
They'd hold it for successive terms
   In several possession.

I wish I had been changed at birth,
   And in my place maturing
Some infant of surpassing worth,
   Industrious past curing,
Had grown up subject to my share
   In Father Adam's blunder,
And left me free to pile up care
   For him to stagger under.

I wish that some things could be had
    Without foregoing others ;
That all the joys that are not bad
    Were not weighed down with bothers.
We can but wonder as we test
    The scheme of compensations,
Is happiness with drawbacks best,
    Or grief with consolations.

TO-DAY.

SEE that what burdens Heaven may lay
    Upon your shrinking neck to day,
        To-day you bear;
Nor seek to shun their weary weight,
Nor, bowed with dread, anticipate
        To-morrow's care.

Not with too great a load shall Fate,
That knows the end, your shoulders freight
        Or heart oppress ;
If but to-day's appointed work
You grapple with, nor wish to shirk
        Its due distress.

The coward heart that turns away
From present tasks, with justice may
        Forebodings fill.
Fools try to quaff to-morrow's wine ;
As though to-morrow's sun could shine
        Unrisen still.

OF MISTRESS MARTHA: HER EYES.

TRANSFIXED and spitted in my heart
   By Mistress Martha's eyes, their dart,
Which has within me raised a great
Commotion and uneasy state.

Or are they black or are they blue
I know not any more than you,
Nor could I for a wager say
If they be hazel, brown or gray.

But when it comes to diagnosis
Of what the outcome of their use is,
Full, comprehensive and exact
Is my conception of the fact.

When first their witchery has begun
You might be saved if you would run;
But who would look for cause for fear
In depths so limpid, calm and clear.
Too soon, poor fool, you find you've stayed
Till it's too late to be afraid.

Alas for him who thus misreckons
For friendly lights mistaking beacons.
Better it were if he had found
Clarence, his fate, in Malmsey drowned,
Than Mistress, in thine eyes to sink,
Nor make a tear o'erflow its brink.

THE BEST GIFT OF ALL.

ONE-AND-TWENTY, one-and-twenty,
Youth and beauty, lovers plenty;
Health and riches, ease and leisure,
Work to give a zest to pleasure;
What can a maid so lucky lack?
What can I wish that Fate holds back?

Youth will fade and beauty wanes;
Lovers, flouted, break their chains.
Health may fail and wealth may fly you,
Pleasures cease to satisfy you;
Almost everything that brings
Happiness is born with wings.

This I wish you—this is best:
Love that can endure the test;
Love surviving youth and beauty,
Love that blends with homely duty,
Love that's gentle, love that's true,
Love that's constant wish I you.

Still unsatisfied she lives
Who for gold mere silver gives.
One more joy I wish you yet,
To give as much love as you get.
Grant you, heaven, this to do,
To love him best who best loves you.

AND WAS HE RIGHT?

" I 'M going to marry—not you," she said,
"But a better fellow in your stead.
You're not so bad—not bad at all;
I'd like to keep you within my call,
But not to take you for good and all.
I'm going to live on yonder street;
Do you live near me," she said; "so sweet
As I'll be to you whenever we meet!
And in my house there'll be a seat
Where you can sit and warm your feet,
And your contentment shall be complete—
Come! Isn't it a divine conceit?"
                              She said.

Softly his breast a sigh set free:
He said, "Dear Heart, it may not be—
Not for the perfume of the rose
Would I live near to where it grows.
If not for me the bud has blown,
I'd rather leave the flower alone;
Who by the bush sits down forlorn
Is only fit to feel the thorn."
                              He said.

AUTUMN.

I HAVE sundry queer sensations
  When the year gets round to Autumn.
What they are, and how I caught 'em
  Is obscure, but they are there—
Certain gay exhilarations
  Half-and-half, as Bass with Guinness,
  With a sad what-might-have-been-ness
  In the brisk September air.

Back come hopes and young ambitions
  With the golden-rod and sumach,
  But impregnated with true Mach-
  Iavellian despair.
Taking note of changed conditions ;
  Weighing powers with limitations !
  Facts with futile aspirations
  Born of bracing autumn air.

Now I see myself grown famous,
  Bold of voice and free of gesture,
  Grave, superb, of stunning vesture
  Flood with eloquence the court.
Soon ascends my *Gaudeamus*
  As I realize there aren't
  Any facts that seem to warrant
  Premonitions of that sort.

Welcome each hallucination:
  Welcome, none the less, discerning
  Common sense in time returning
    To obliterate the spell.
As a means of elevation—
  As a sort of moral derrick
  This autumnal, atmospheric
    Spirit-hoister bears the bell.

TOUCHING BOTTOM.

I THINK that I have somewhere read
  About a man whose foolish head,
By mischievous intention led,
          A sprite
Had with an ass's visage decked,
That all who met him might detect
His intellectual defect
          At sight

The trite remark of man and book
That many men are men in look,
But donkeys really, thus the spook
          Reversed ;
The victim of the imp's design
Had such a head as yours or mine,
Although in aspect asinine
          At first.

But Love—I think the story ran—
Was proof against the fairy's plan,
Discerning through the mask the man,
                    Perhaps;
Or, is it true that women try,
But very faintly, to descry
Long ears on heads that occupy
                    Their laps!

I know a youth whose fancy gropes
For headgear finer than the Pope's,
So him his bright and treacherous hopes
                    Delude;
But, in the mirror of his fears,
When this too sanguine person peers,
Alas! behold the jackass ears
                    Protrude!

Titania, mine, if I could find
You always to my follies blind,
So great content would rule my mind
                    Within,
That even though myself aware
Of pointed ears adorned with hair,
I do not think that I would care
                    A pin.

IN THE ELYSIAN FIELDS.

WHAT? You here! Why, old man, I never
    Felt more surprise or more delight;
Who would have dreamt that you would ever
    Parade around in robes of white?
I always thought of you as dodging
    The coals and firebrands somewhere else;
And here you are, with board and lodging,
    Where not so much as butter melts.

Well, well, old man, if you can stand it
    Up here, I'll never make a fuss;
I had forebodings that they'd planned it
    A little stiff for men like us.
The boys were much cut up about you,
    You got away so very quick;
And, as for me, to do without you
    Just absolutely made me sick.

I wish you could have seen us plant you;
    Why, every man squeezed out a tear,
And—just imagine us, now, can't you?—
    The gang, and yours the only bier.
Fred hammered out some bully verses;
    We had them printed in the sheet,
With lines funereal as hearses
    Around them—didn't it look sweet!

Halloo! is that Sir Walter Raleigh?—
    I wish you'd point the people out;
I want to look at Tom Macaulay;
    Is Makepeace anywhere about?

Where's Socrates? Where's Sydney Carton?—
    Oh, I forgot he was a myth;
If there's a thing I've set my heart on
    It is to play with Sidney Smith.

What? Glad I came? I am for certain;
    The other's a malarious hole.
I always pined to draw the curtain,
    And somehow knew I had a soul.
The flesh—oh, wasn't it a fetter!
    You'd get so tired of all your schemes;
But here, I think, I'll like it better.
    Oh dear, how natural it seems!

———

ET TU, BERGHE!

AND art thou, Bergh, so firmly set
    Against domestic strife,
As to correct with stripes the man
    Who disciplines his wife?

Such action doth not of thy creed
    Appear the normal fruit;
Thou shouldst befriend a being who
    Behaves so like a brute!

REMORSE.

M Y spirit sits in ashes, heaping dust upon its head ;
I've said a silly thing, and now it cannot be unsaid.
What boots it that to only two the wretched truth is known,
If of the conscious pair who know it I myself am one ?

I have my doubts—more doubts the more I think of what I said—
If, really, half a loaf is so much better than no bread ;
For if a person is an ass, and duly bound to show it,
Cold comfort 'tis that he should have just sense enough to
know it.

HONI SOIT QUI MAL Y PENSE.

IT was my happy lot to meet
  Upon a late occasion,
While seeking of the summer's heat
  Agreeable evasion,
By visiting at a resort
  Of fashion—where, no matter—
A maid whom there was none to court,
  And very few to flatter.

Her head had not the graceful poise
  Of Aphrodite's statue;
Her hair reminded you of boys;
  Her nose was pointed at you.
A Derby hat, the selfsame sort
  The fashionable male owes
Money for, she used to sport
  As angels do their haloes.

She seldom walked in silk attire,
  But commonly in flannel;
Nor yet in oils did she aspire
  To figure on a panel;
Because she could not help but see
  She was not tall, nor slender;
Nor did she deem her curves to be
  Superlatively tender.

Some prudish dames did her abuse
  With censure fierce and scathing;
Because she, happening to lose
  Her stocking while in bathing;

Deemed such a loss of little note.
 And simply tied the plagued
Stocking around her little throat
 And reappeared barelegged.

I do not think that for the pelf
 Of eligible boobies,
Or for the chance to deck herself
 With diamonds and rubies,
Or for her standing in the books
 Of prim and proper ladies.
Or for their disapproving looks,
 She cared a hoot from Hades.

Though competent to hold her tongue,
 When circumstance demanded
Speech, she was, for one so young,
 Astonishingly candid.
She sang the vulgarest of songs,
 Which sung by her were funny,
And never brooded o'er her wrongs—
 Nor hoarded up her money.

'Tis true this careless damsel's fame
 At last grew somewhat shady ;
But if the man disposed to name
 Her fast, or not a lady,
Will in the present writer's way
 Considerately toddle,
This writer thinks that person may
 Get punched upon his noddle.

CIVIL SERVICE.

ON Pennsylvania avenue
    He stood and waited for a car ;
He turned to catch a parting view
    Of where the Public Buildings are :
He looked at them with thoughtful eye ;
    He took his hat from off his head ;
He heaved a half-regretful sigh,
    And thus he said :

" My relative, I do the bidding
    Of Fate, and say to thee good-bye.
I think thee fortunate at ridding
    Thyself of such a clerk as I.
Thy sure support, though somewhat meagre,
    Hath much about it to commend ;
Nor am I now so passing eager
    To leave so provident a friend.

Light was thy yoke could I have borne it
    With tranquil mind and step sedate ;
Why did my feeble shoulders scorn it
    And seem to crave a heavier weight ?
Extremely blest is his condition
    Whose needs thy bounteous hands supply,
If he but fling away ambition
    And let the world go rushing by.

Indocilis pauperiem pati,
    I must get out of this damp spot.
Away ! away ! Whatever fate I
    May have in store, I fear it not.

33

Away from all my soul despises,
  From paltry aims, from sordid cares;
Fame, honor, love, time's richest prizes,
  Lie waiting for the man who dares.

The man who calls no man his master
  Nor bows his head to tinsel gods;
Who faces debt, disease, disaster,
  And never murmurs at the odds;
Although his life from its beginning
  Marks only fall succeeding fall,
Let him fight on and trust to winning
  In death the richest prize of all."

He jammed his hat down on his head,
  He turned from where the Buildings are;
Precipitately thence he fled,
  And caught a passing car.

A PHILADELPHIA CLAVERHOUSE.

TO the fathers in council 'twas Witherspoon spoke:
" Our best beloved dogmas we cannot revoke;
God's infinite mercy let others record
And teach men to trust in their crucified Lord ;
The old superstitions let others dispel,
I feel it my duty to go in for Hell !

Perdition is needful ; beyond any doubt
Hell fire is a thing that we can't do without.
The bottomless pit is our very best claim ;
To leave it unworked were a sin and a shame ;
We *must* keep it up, if we like it or not,
And make it eternal and make it red-hot.

To others the doctrine of love may be dear—
I own I confide in the doctrine of fear ;
There's nothing, I think, so effective to make
Our weak fellow mortals their errors forsake,
As to tell them abruptly, with unchanging front,
' You'll be damned if you do ! You'll be damned if you don't !'

Saltpetre and pitchforks, with brimstone and coals,
Are arguments suited to rescue men's souls.
A new generation forthwith must arise
With Beelzebub pictured before their young eyes ;
They'll be brave, they'll be true, they'll be gentle and kind,
Because they'll have Satan forever in mind."

A MORTIFYING SUBJECT.

WHAT is to be, I do not know:
   What is, I do esteem
To be so undesirable
   And worthless, that I deem
There must be something good in store,
   Something to keep in view,
To compensate us living here,
   For living as we do.

For life—oh life, it seems a chore !
   Its surface is so blurred
By cares and passions, that it makes
   One long to be interred;
To occupy a tranquil spot
   Some seven feet by two,
And just serenely lie and rot,
   With nothing else to do.

I think that when there ceased to be
   Sufficient tenement
To hold my conscience, then I would
   Begin to be content.
And if I should be there to see
   My stomach take its leave,
I'd gather up my mouldering shroud
   And chuckle in my sleeve.

I think that when the greedy worm
   Began upon my brains,
I'd wish him luck, and hope he'd get
   His dinner for his pains.

I'd warn him that they would be apt
    With him to disagree,
For if they fed him well 'twere what
    They seldom did for me.

But when I should be certain that
    My scarred and battered heart
Was of my corporality
    Not any more a part,
Though I'd no voice, I'd rattle in
    My throat, with joyous tones ;
And with no feelings left, I would
    Feel happy in my bones.

WHAT HE WANTS IN HIS.

I DO not ask thee, Fate, to bake
　For me so very large a cake ;
Choose thou the size—but I entreat
That though but small, it shall be sweet.
　　Let those who like it have it, I
　　Feel no desire for sawdust pie.

I have no wail for all the years
I've lived on crusts washed down with tears.
If I must drain the bitter cup
As heretofore, why—fill it up.
　　But when my cake, if ever, comes,
　　Vouchsafe it to me full of plums.

MIXED.

WITHIN my earthly temple there's a crowd.
　There's one of us that's humble ; one that's proud.
There's one that's broken-hearted for his sins,
And one who, unrepentant, sits and grins.
There's one who loves his neighbor as himself,
And one who cares for naught but fame and pelf.
From much corroding care I would be free
If once I could determine which is me.

ALL OR NOTHING.

HAPPY the man whose far remove
    From business and the giddy throng
Fits him in the paternal groove
    Unquestioning to glide along.
Apart from struggle and from strife,
    Content to live by labor's fruits,
And wander down the vale of life
    In gingham shirt and cowhide boots,

He too is blessed who, from within,
    By strong and lasting impulse stirred,
Faces the turmoil and the din
    Of rushing life ; whom hope deferred
But more incites ; who ever strives,
    And wants, and works, and waits, until
The multitude of other lives
    Pay glorious tribute to his will.

But he who, greedy of renown,
    Is too tenacious of his ease,
Alas for him ! Nor busy town
    Nor country with his mood agrees ;
Eager to reap, but loath to sow,
He longs *monstrari digito*,
And looking on with envious eyes,
Lives restless and obscurely dies.

PROCUL NEGOTIIS.

I THINK that if I had a farm,
  I'd be a man of sense;
And if the day was bright and warm
  I'd sit upon the fence,
And calmly smoke a pensive pipe
  And think about my pigs;
And wonder if the corn was ripe;
  And counsel *l'homme qui* digs.

And if the day was wet and cold,
  I think I should admire
To sit, and dawdle over old
  Montaigne, before the fire;
And pity boobies who could lie
  And squabble just for pelf;
And thank my blessed stars that I
  Was comfortable myself.

EPITHALAMIUM.

THE marriage bells have rung their peal,
  The wedding march has told its story.
I've seen her at the altar kneel
  In all her stainless, virgin glory;
She's bound to honor, love, obey,
  Come joy or sorrow, tears or laughter.
I watched her as she rode away
  And flung the lucky slipper after.

She was my first, my very first,
  My earliest inamorata,
And to the passion that I nursed
  For her I well-nigh was a martyr.
For I was young and she was fair,
  And always bright and gay and chipper,
And, oh, she wore such sunlit hair!
  Such silken stockings! such a slipper!

She did not wish to make me mourn—
  She was the kindest of God's creatures;
But flirting was in her inborn,
  Like brains and queerness in the Beechers.
I do not fear your heartless flirt,
  Obtuse her dart and dull her probe is;
But when girls do not mean to hurt,
  But *do—Orate tunc pro nobis!*

A most romantic country place;
  The moon at full, the month of August;
An inland lake across whose face
  Played gentle zephyrs, ne'er a raw gust.
Books, boats and horses to enjoy,
  The which was all our occupation;
A damsel and a callow boy—
  There! now you have the situation.

We rode together miles and miles,
  My pupil she, and I her Chiron;
At home I reveled in her smiles
  And read her extracts out of Byron.
We roamed by moonlight, chose our stars
  (I thought it most authentic billing),
Explored the woods, climbed over bars,
  Smoked cigarettes and broke a shilling.

An infinitely blissful week
  Went by in this Arcadian fashion;
I hesitated long to speak,
  But ultimately breathed my passion.
She said her heart was not her own;
  She said she'd love me like a sister;
She cried a little (not alone),
  I begged her not to fret, and—kissed her.

I lost some sleep, some pounds in weight,
  A deal of time and all my spirits,
And much, how much I dare not state
  I mused upon that damsel's merits.
I tortured my unhappy soul,
  I wished I never might recover;

I hoped her marriage bells might toll
  A requiem for her faithful lover.

And now she's married, now she wears
  A wedding ring upon her finger;
And I—although it odd appears—
  Still in the flesh I seem to linger.
Lo, there my swallow-tail, and here
  Lies by my side a wedding favor;
Beside it stands a mug of beer,
  I taste it—how divine its flavor!

I saw her in her bridal dress
  Stand pure and lovely at the altar;
I heard her firm response—that "Yes,"
  Without a quiver or a falter.
And here I sit and drink to her
  Long life and happiness, God bless her!
Now fill again.   No heel taps, sir;
  Here's to—Success to her successor!

AGAIN.

I WONDER why my brow is burning;
 Why sleep, to close my eyes forgets ;
I wonder why I have a yearning
 To smoke incessant cigarettes.
I wonder why my thoughts will wander,
 And all restraint of mine defy,
And why—excuse the rhyme—a gander
 Is not more of a goose than I.

I have an indistinct impression
 I had these symptoms once before,
And dull discomfort held possession
 Of this same spot that now is sore.
That sometime in a past that ranges
 From early whiskers up to bibs,
My heart was ringing just such changes
 As now against these selfsame ribs.

I wish some philanthropic Jenner
 Might vaccinate against these ills,
And help us keep our noiseless tenor
 Of life submissive to our wills ;
And ere our hearts are permeated
 By sentiments too warm by half,
That we might be inoculated
 With milder passion from a calf.

MEA CULPA.

THERE is a thing which in my brain,
    Though nightly I revolve it,
I cannot in the least explain,
    Nor do I hope to solve it.
While others tread the narrow path
    In manner meek and pious,
Why is it that my spirit hath
    So opposite a bias?

Brought up to fear the Lord, and dread
    The bottomless abysm,
In Watt's hymns profoundly read
    And drilled in catechism,
I should have been a model youth,
    The pink of all that's proper.
I was not, but—to tell the truth—
    I never cared a copper.

I had no yearnings when a boy
    To sport an angel's wrapper,
Nor heard I with tumultuous joy
    The church-frequenting clapper.
My actions always harmonized
    With my own sweet volition.
I always did what I devised.
    But rarely asked permission.

When o'er the holy book I'd pore
    And read of doings pristine,
I had a fellow-feeling for
    The put-upon Philistine.

King David gratified my taste—
   He harped and danced boleros ;
But first the Prodigal was placed
   Upon my list of heroes.

I went to school. To study ? No !
   I dearly loved to dally
And dawdle over Ivanhoe,
   Tom Brown and Charles O'Malley ;
In recitation I was used
   To halt on every sentence ;
Repenting, seldom I produced
   Fruits proper for repentance.

At college, later, I became
   Familiar with my Flaccus,
Brought incense to the Muses' flame,
   And sacrificed to Bacchus.
I flourished in an air unfraught
   With sanctity's aroma ;
Learned many things I was not taught,
   And captured a diploma.

I am not well provided for,
   I have no great possessions,
I do not like the legal or
   Medicinal professions.
Were I of good repute, I might
   Take orders as a deacon ;
But I'm no bright and shining light,
   But just a warning beacon.

Though often urged by friends sincere
   To woo some funded houri,

I cannot read my title clear
    To any damsel's dowry.
And could to wedlock I induce
    An heiress, I should falter,
For fear that such a bridal noose
    Might prove a gilded halter.

My tradesmen have suspicious grown,
    My friends are tired of giving;
Upon the cold, cold world I'm thrown
    To hammer out my living.
I fear that work before me lies—
    Indeed, I see no option,
Unless, perhaps, I advertise—
    " An orphan for adoption!"

TO MABEL.

UPON this anniversar*ee*,
    My little godchild, aged three,
My compliments I make to thee,
      Quite heedless.
And that you'll throw them now away,
But treasure them some future day,
Are platitudes, the which to say
      Is needless.

You small, stout damsel, muckle mou'd,
With cropped tow-head and manners rude,
And stormy spirit unsubdued
      By nurses.
Where you were raised was it in vogue
To lisp that Tipperary brogue?
Oh, you're a subject sweet, you rogue,
      For verses !

Last Sunday morning when we stayed
At home you got yourself arrayed
In Lyman's clothes and turned from maid
      To urchin.
And when we all laughed at you so,
You eyed outside the falling snow,
And thought your rig quite fit to go
      To church in.

Play on, play on, dear little lass !
Play on till sixteen summers pass,
And then I'll bring a looking-glass,
    And there be-
Fore you on your lips I'll show
The curves of small Dan Cupid's bow,
And then the crop that now is " tow "
    Shall " fair " be.

And then I'll show you, too, the charms
Of small firm hands and rounded arms,
And eyes whose flashes send alarms
    Right through you ;
And then a half-regretful sigh
May break from me to think that I,
At forty years, can never try
    To woo you.

What shall I wish you ? Free from ruth,
To live and learn in love and truth,
Through childhood's day and days of youth,
    And school's day.
For all the days that intervene
'Twixt Mab at three and at nineteen,
Are but one sombre or serene
    All Fools' Day.

LOCHINVAR EX-COLORADO.

OH, the cow-puncher Budge has come in from the West;
    In all Colorado his ranch is the best;
And, barring a toothbrush, he baggage had none,
For he came in some haste, and he came not for fun;
Nor vigils nor gold to his quest doth he grudge—
On an errand of love comes the cow-puncher Budge.

A telegram reached him ; he called for a horse.
He rode ninety miles as a matter of course :
The last twenty-seven he galloped, and then
Just caught the Atlantic Express at Cheyenne.
He stayed not to eat nor to drink, for he knew
He could pick up a meal on the C. B. & Q.

He got to Chicago the second day out,
But right through Chicago he kept on his route,
Nor stayed to buy linen, not even a shirt ;
He liked flannel best and he didn't mind dirt.
With trousers tucked into his boots, said he " Fudge !—
Small odds—if I get there," said bold Robert Budge.

* * * * * * *

From Worth, the Parisian of awful repute,
Had come divers gowns to Angelica Bute,
And parcels from Tiffany daily were stowed
Away in strong rooms of her father's abode ;
But she languished, nor heeded she hint, cough or nudge :
She was bound to Fitz James, but she cottoned to Budge.

But hark ! 'Tis the door-bell ! a symptom of joy
Lights her eye—" Ah ! at last !" 'Tis a telegraph boy :
The maid brings a message ; she takes it, half dead
With mingled excitement, hope, eagerness—dread :
*"Mayor's house on Thursday, at nine; let me judge
What next ; only meet me there.*

       Faithfully,

         Budge."

* * * * * * *

On Thursday at nine, to the house of the Mayor,
Two persons came singly, but left it a pair.
A man and a bride in a traveling dress,
Went Westward at ten on the lightning express.
A wedding at Grace Church, which should have occurred
At twelve, was, for reasons not given, deferred.

The dowagers called it the greatest of shames.
The men said, " It's rough on that fellow Fitz James : "
The damsels declared it was awfully nice,
And vowed they could do it and never think twice.
" It's a chore to get housemaids ; you may have to drudge
At the start ; but—I love you," said cow-puncher Budge.